ACROSS THREE CONTINENTS: THE LEGACY OF ANTOINETTE FERNANDES

CARMELITO ANDRADE

NICOLE SUARES

MARIUS FERNANDES

Copyright © Carmelito Andrade,Nicole Suares, Marius Fernandes
All Rights Reserved.

This book has been self-published with all reasonable efforts taken to make the material error-free by the author. No part of this book shall be used, reproduced in any manner whatsoever without written permission from the author, except in the case of brief quotations embodied in critical articles and reviews.

The Author of this book is solely responsible and liable for its content including but not limited to the views, representations, descriptions, statements, information, opinions and references ["Content"]. The Content of this book shall not constitute or be construed or deemed to reflect the opinion or expression of the Publisher or Editor. Neither the Publisher nor Editor endorse or approve the Content of this book or guarantee the reliability, accuracy or completeness of the Content published herein and do not make any representations or warranties of any kind, express or implied, including but not limited to the implied warranties of merchantability, fitness for a particular purpose. The Publisher and Editor shall not be liable whatsoever for any errors, omissions, whether such errors or omissions result from negligence, accident, or any other cause or claims for loss or damages of any kind, including without limitation, indirect or consequential loss or damage arising out of use, inability to use, or about the reliability, accuracy or sufficiency of the information contained in this book.

Made with ♥ on the Notion Press Platform
www.notionpress.com

Contents

Acknowledgements   *v*

Dedication   *vii*

Message from the Publisher   *ix*

Author's Note 1   *xi*

Author's Note 2   *xiii*

Caricature - by ALEXYZ   *xvii*

1. Introduction   1

2. The Incredible Life Of Antoinette   11

3. 'Our Hero' -Recollections Of A Loving Mother And Grandmother   39

4. Notes From Friends   51

5. Sing Along   64

6. Recipes   69

A Book For Mum on Her Birthday   73

Acknowledgements

We owe a special thanks to our proofreaders - Linguist Dona Lucia Fatima Zito de Ornelas and Senior Journalist Govind Potekar, who have painfully gone through the book multiple times .

We would like to express our deepest gratitude to our publisher Dr. Gwendolyn de Ornelas, for her invaluable guidance and financial support throughout the process of this book.

Photos in the book were taken over a period of time by the authors Marius Fernandes and Carmelito Andrade.

We are also thankful to Akshay Mahajan for the concept of the front cover of the book.

Dedication

For as long as I can remember, my mother, Antoinette Fernandes, has been a storyteller. Her life—spanning three continents and decades of change—has been filled with experiences that shaped not only her journey but also mine. Through her, I learned about our Goan heritage, the struggles and triumphs of our ancestors, and the importance of preserving our culture and traditions.

However, I have also seen how quickly stories can fade. In Goa, much of our history has been passed down orally—from generation to generation—through conversations, songs, recipes, and traditions. But as time moves forward, these stories risk being lost. I realized that if we do not take the initiative to document the lives of our elders, we will lose a vital part of our identity.

I wanted this book to be written not just as a tribute to my mother but as an example for every Goan family. This is not just her story—it is the story of many Goans, a reflection of the experiences, values, and resilience that define our community. I believe every family has a history worth preserving, whether through written records, photographs, audio recordings, or digital archives.

Over the years, my mother's wisdom and stories have influenced my own path. Inspired by her, I have dedicated my life to curating and organizing over 100 people's festivals across Goa as part of my individual social responsibility. These festivals celebrate our history, traditions, music, food, and way of life, ensuring that our cultural heritage remains relevant and accessible to all. But beyond festivals, I realized that true preservation begins at home—with families documenting their own stories.

Goa is changing fast. With rapid modernization, migration, and the loss of traditional ways of life, we risk losing the essence of what makes Goa unique. The least we can do is ensure that our family histories—our roots—are not forgotten.

This book has been brought to life through the dedication of renowned freelance journalist Nicole Suares, who spent over a year documenting my mother's journey, and has been published with the support of our close family friend, Dr. Gwendolyn de Ornelas from Loutolim.

I hope that when you read this book, you are not only inspired by my mother's journey but also feel a sense of urgency to begin chronicling your own family's story. Our history is not just found in textbooks or archives—it lives in the hearts and memories of our elders. If we do not document it, we risk losing an irreplaceable part of who we are.

Let this book serve as a reminder that the past is not something to be forgotten—it is something to be preserved and cherished. Together, let us ensure that the voices of our ancestors continue to echo through time, one family story at a time.

Festacar Marius Fernandes

Son, Curator, Festival Director

Message From The Publisher

"Mhojea mogall Anna ani Goenkar ixtt,"

It is an honour to present the extraordinary life and times of *Dona* Anna Regina—a woman of wisdom, resilience, and grace whose journey has spanned three continents. This endeavor seeks to capture the depth of her experiences and the indelible mark she has left on those around her.

It is an honour to present the extraordinary life and times of *Dona* Anna Regina—a woman of wisdom, resilience, and grace whose journey has spanned three continents. This endeavor seeks to capture the depth of her experiences and the indelible mark she has left on those around her.

Over the past few years, I have had the privilege of knowing *Dona* Anna as a dear friend—celebrating life with her, learning invaluable lessons, and immersing myself in the rich tapestry of her experiences. Born into a Brahmin (Bamonn) family, our cultures met with her legacy of tradition and heritage.

Sharing the same heritage, I am honored to be the publisher of my *Querida* Anna's book—a masterpiece and a vision brought to life by her eldest son, *Festacar* Marius.

The daughter, my close friend, Maria Goretti Conçeicâo and *Festacar* Marius are always up to keeping the family together. I admire the *Festacar's* children, Ashley and Gemma, who are proud of their roots.

This book stands as a testament to the importance of documenting one's family history—a remarkable endeavor every family should undertake.

Beyond her personal journey, Dona Anna's life has profoundly shaped her son, Festacar Marius, whose remarkable contributions to Goan culture include organizing over 100 peoples' festivals across Goa. Rooted in his mother's legacy and the lessons of the past, he has played a pivotal role in reviving cultural heritage, earning him the affectionate title of the Festival Man of Goa. In my knowledge, there are two figures who have left an unforgettable impact on Goa: *Goencho Saib* - St. Francis Xavier, who I have religious faith in and *Goencho Festacar* - Marius Fernandes.

This book is more than a tribute to a life well lived—it is a chronicle of history, culture and family.

Our family proverbs:

"A família é uma das obras-primas da natureza."
"Para bom entendedor, meia palavra basta."

Dr. Gwendolyn de Ornelas

Loutolim, Goa

Author's Note 1

Putting this book together was challenging for all the authors and more rewarding than we ever imagined.

It was an honor meeting Festacar Marius Fernandes' Mum - Antoinette Fernandes. The highlight for me was listening to some of her stories from her time in Kenya and the United Kingdom. And Yes ! her love for Goa. Like my own father, she is also a big proponent of Konkani. Her opinion has been that every Goan living in Goa or overseas should speak konkani at home. A forceful statement that stayed with me -

> *" Mhozo vell zalo, haven zata toxem amchi Goenchi bhas ani tradição sambailem, ata konkani sambalpak ani Goeche sanskar rakpak, tumi bhurgeani fuddem sorpak zai mhun axetam"*

Carmelito Andrade - Nuvem, Salcete - 2025

Author's Note 2

In the American Christian drama film *Unsung Hero*, a mother's unwavering faith guides her family through life's storms. It traces the Smallbones family's journey from the collapse of the father's music company in Australia to their new life in America and the subsequent success of their children. It is a tribute to Helen, the mother's steadfast faith through their tough times.

A mother's sacrifice often goes unnoticed. The media constantly bombards us with celebrity headlines and gossip, often leaving our everyday heroes in the shadows.

This book aims to celebrate these silent champions who shape our lives. Antoinette Fernandes is one such mother. She embodies every mother who has loved, toiled, and sacrificed for her family. She is our unsung hero. Her remarkable journey, breaking barriers before the women's emancipation movement of the 60s, makes her an inspiration.

What's striking about her story is her steadfast love for Goa wherever she travelled, the resilience to face the dangers of her new life in Africa, and the uncertainties of bringing her children back to Divar in 1968.

She preserved Konkani through her travels with unwavering dedication, passing her love for the language to her children. She found ways to connect with the Goan community, offering support and generosity to those in need.

This book is a 'Thank You' to a mother, sister, friend, neighbour, and a true Goan.

It's an honor and a privilege knowing Aunty Antoinette over the years through her son Marius, Goa's renowned *Festacar*. I'm continually amazed by Marius's tireless efforts in his eco-friendly festivals, and my visits to their home in St. Mathias have been enriched by the presence of his dear mother.

Her life is filled with wisdom, and our conversations strengthen my connection to home. Our shared love for Goa rekindles the simple values deeply rooted in Goan culture. Through our balcony chats, I'm transported back to childhood summers on cashew-laden hills, to the cosmopolitan lifestyle of a Goan family in the UK, and to the importance of returning to one's roots.

It started as a small publication for her 92nd birthday and evolved into a larger project due to the overwhelming response. I thank Marius for helping gather information through the interviews with Antoinette, sourcing information from friends, and other research. I am grateful to Dr. Gwendolyn de Ornelas for her generosity in helping bring this idea to fruition as its publisher. My heartfelt thanks go to both for their faith in me as I wrote this book.

Aunty Antoinette is a testament to the enduring values that shape a fulfilled life. While the millennial generation may often be distracted by fleeting likes and swipes on an app, we can learn much from the older generation.

It is a true pleasure to embark on my journey as an author with a mother's blessings. Her welcoming smile and warm hospitality embody the true Goan spirit that continues to thrive today.

Nicole Suares - Panjim, 2025

Caricature - By Alexyz

Caricature by ALEXYZ, Goa's ace cartoonist and friend of the family.

CHAPTER ONE

Introduction

DIVAR, 2024

The ferry from the Ribandar jetty glides gently across the calm waters of the River Mandovi, heading towards Divar (*Divaddi*) Island. It is the third largest island in North Goa, nestled between two tributaries of the River Mandovi and is about 10 kilometers from Panjim's bustling main KTC bus terminus,

As the ferry drifts past the Ribandar riverbank, or *Rayachem Bandar* (Docks of Kings), the striking façade of the former *Santa Casa de Misericórdia*, or Holy House of Charity, comes into view. Once Asia's oldest medical college, this historical gem reminds one of the Portuguese legacy. However, the stark reality of the modern concrete structures perched on the Kadamba Plateau tells of the present reality facing Goa.

Turning slowly, the ferry faces the neighboring islands of Chorão and Divar. The mangroves, home to the famous Salim Ali Bird Sanctuary, lining Chorão's perimeter come into sight. It attracts a diverse array of Indian avian life.

Gone with the Storm: The iconic mango tree no longer watches over the passers-by.

On arrival at the Divar dock, the crisp, fresh island air offers a welcome embrace. Change has quietly settled into this once-sleepy island. The first is the missing mango tree, a landmark for centuries that once stood a few kilometers from the pier. It gained fame after being featured in the Bollywood film *"Finding Fenny"*.

Hidden in vegetation, out of sight, is another forgotten treasure the *"Dovodnnem"*, a rectangular stone platform once used by travelers in the past to rest their heavy loads.

The peaceful drive through the narrow road alongside the green pastures carries your gaze to the towering monuments of St. Augustine's Tower and Se Cathedral dotting the horizon. Tourists whizz past on rented bikes, following their GPS maps to Insta-worthy locations.

The journey bends through picturesque island wards—Piedade, divided into Goltim, Navelim, and São Mathias (Malar)—each adorned with vibrant Goan heritage homes. These postcard-worthy vistas showcase the authentic Goan charm that cannot be found anywhere else.

The island's diverse terrain creates a textured landscape, featuring verdant hillocks that lead to the low-lying traditional agricultural Khazan lands, carpeted with rolling fields and local vegetable patches. The River Mandovi feeds the small canals where locals operate their small boats.

Depending on the time of day, the unmistakable call of the cuckoo pierces through the foliage. Occasionally, an egret or two will land on the wharf, observing the ferry as it departs. In the evenings, the sluice gates (*manos*) attract local fishermen who throw in their rods or nets, hopeful to catch local varieties like the striped grey mullet, prawns, crabs, Kalundora.

North of Divar lies the islet of Vanxim, which falls under Malar's administrative jurisdiction. Naroa is the third ward (communidade) of the island.

Divar is steeped in history dating before the Portuguese. The ancient Ganesh temple and the site remains of the Saptakoteshwar temple are signs of its rich heritage.

It is said that the original islanders hailed from Old Goa, Velha Goa and the old capital before it moved to Panjim, after the plague.

Dotting the countryside are the beautiful white-washed 400-plus old churches. The beautiful hillside Church of Our Lady of Piety overlooks Piedade with panoramic views of Divar and the surrounding areas.

The late Fr. Jacome Gonsalves, known for his missionary work in Ceylon and regarded as a saint in the making, is one of the famous sons from Piedade. Leading entrepreneurs like CMM Menezes and intellectuals such as poet, writer and academician Armando Menezes hail from São Mathias.

Legendary musicians like Anibal Crasto, a trombonist from Mumbai and Lucilla Pacheco, a pioneering pianist known for introducing the Solovox, the first electronic keyboard in Hindi films, draw their roots to Malar. Renowned MAGs and Helen's hairdressers from Panjim are from the island.

Another famed resident of Malar is Goa's beloved *festacar*, Marius Fernandes. His innovative, inclusive, sponsor-free green festivals have revived Goa's forgotten traditions.

The Fernandes home in the village is perched atop one of the hilly slopes of Malar, behind the São Mathias Sports Club. Nestled in the cozy by-lane of *Amboi Waddo*, the white façade stands out as ancient Goan earthen percussions (*ghumots*) hanging from the rafters add to the eye-catching decor. The *ghumots* occupy a significant place in the household due to Marius's tireless work saving the instrument from extinction.

On the balcony (*balcão*), Marius's mother, Ana Regina Antoinette Fernandes, affectionately called Antoinette, sits in an old wicker chair. Dressed in a simple cotton dress with her hair neatly tied back, her gracious smile warmly welcomes everyone who enters their gate.

Balcão Chat: Flory, Anton and Philu exchange stories with Antoinette.

At 92, it is hard to believe that Antoinette's memory remains sharp with vivid details of a Goa that few remember these days. Mention her age, and she playfully retorts, "Only!" with a chuckle, never missing an opportunity to keep her sense of humor intact.

Marius, who's always been close to her sits next to her, helping her jog her memory for interesting nuggets from her past. A little coaxing reveals interesting notes about the in-laws' family history. The Fernandes', she says, are known as the Grão family in Divar. It is believed that their great-grandfather, *Moti* Xavier Fernandes, earned the title after he generously distributed grams (*chonne*) to everyone he met on his return from a feast on the mainland.

(left) The *Festacar* name features in an old Souvenir (right) A holy picture given after a chapel feast celebrated by the family.

The Fernandes' family connection to the Festacar name dates back to an old Malar Sports Club souvenir from 1989-1990 that refers to the entire family by this name. Another old holy picture mentions the family celebrating the feast at the *Nossa Senhora dos Agonisantes* chapel in their ward (*waddo)* on May 1, 1933.

The chapel was built in 1916. The family later commemorated the 400th anniversary of São Mathias Church.

A conversation with Antoinette uncovers the extraordinary life of a woman who has lived across three continents. She carved her path in many ways. From the wild African bush in Laare, Kenya, where she put her entrepreneurial skills to the test, to forging a new life in England, she has lived a rich and challenging life.

Growing up in 1930s Goa, Antoinette recalls a forgotten Goa. She delights in sharing stories of her beloved *Adlem Goem* (the Goa of yesteryears) with heritage enthusiasts, family and neighbors. She effortlessly moves between the decades, recalling her time as a young actress in village *tiatrs* and reliving her wedding in Old Goa in 1958.

Her stories have spread far beyond her balcony in Divar through the video interviews with Marius posted on his Facebook. Her witty remarks and infectious laughter have caught the attention of the global Goan diaspora and stirreda deep sense of nostalgia.

Comments pour in on each video as they strike a fond memory. When Marius and mum discussed the use of *mollam* (a technique of interweaving the palm fronds) as a barrier for the rains, one fan, Marcilia Rodrigues - comments on the video :

"I enjoy the way you involve your mum in your videos. She must be loving it. She's the real star of the show. It's good for her to remember when this was the only way to protect the balcão from rain and winds. Now, everyone uses blue plastic sheets, which look ugly. "

Audrey C. James recalls how her mother also spoke of the *mollam* raincoat. Aparna Laad applauds the preservation of the 'old, eco-friendly traditions.'

In addition to revisiting the past, she shares her thoughts on current issues, like the ongoing debate over the proposed bridge linking Divar to the mainland. Antoinette expresses concerns that such a development could increase robberies on the island.

The videos are well appreciated. Writer and Principal of Goa College of Arts Willy Goes, who actively journeys with the mother-son duo through their online videos, highlights the importance of such an exercise.

"Marius is attached to his mother and lovingly records many aspects of Goa through his mother. The old songs and recollections about her life in Africa and Goa all become part of oral history. We will not get it anywhere else," he says.

He regrets not doing the same with his mother, who would share details of the past from St Estevam Island.

Antoinette often surprises viewers with old Konkani numbers (*cantaram*) and hymns like *Sant Anton* and *Ankvar Marie*. Swahili songs like *Harambe, Harambe,* and *Jumbo Jumbo* flow melodiously.

Antoinette at the *Ostoreanchem Fest* in Madkai on 14/6/2023 where she regaled visitors with a song. (Top) Maria Goretti, Maria Fatima, Angela Valadares, Marius and (right) Fr. Gabriel Coutinho.

Coax her to sing, and the songbird doesn't hesitate. Her voice, still on the pitch, carries the lyrics in perfect rhythm to *Dhalia.* At the 2023 *Ostoreachem Fest* in Madkai, Antoinette entertained the visitors with the late Alexin de Candolim's tribute to the late great Konkani *tiatrist* Minguel Rod's, *Chouter Outumbrache.* Although she first sang it in Salvador do Mundo (Saloi) in 1956, she knew it all.

If music makes a Goan's heart strike a happy chord, food unites the Goan family. Antoinette's kitchen stories have helped her children revive old recipes.

Old Goan delicacies like *doce bhaji* and methods for traditional Goan sausages are reproduced after a slight jog to her sharp memory. She even attempted a healthier version of the *sanna* (a steamed rice cake) using *urad dal* and fruit as a natural sweetener. Ask her about a preparation using *shevte* (mullet, the State fish of Goa), and she offers the option of frying it with stuffing or turning it into a delicious curry.

She's got a ready recipe for *molle*, or dry prawns.

'First, you clean it; remove the black thread (*sutli*) from the spine and leave it to dry in the sun. You can put it on a coal fire or fry it with little oil on the frying pan.'

She still assists with the meals. Some days, she assists in cleaning fresh vegetables or keeps a watchful eye on the help.

Dusk settles, and silence envelops the island. The devout Catholic maintains a fervent prayer life she has followed since childhood. She says her daily rosary consistently at 8:30 PM, right before dinner.

Her memories weave through the timeline of her extraordinary journey. Her motivating life has inspired everyone she has met along her journey. Antoinette's connection to the land and its culture runs deep. She says, "I was born and raised in the village and worked in our fields and hills in Saloi. I have a deep connection with the land. I grew up savoring the most exotic fruits, baked cakes and bread, harvested cashews and seeds and brewed alcohol. When I was abroad, I missed these amazing activities. Goa is heaven."

A visit to the Pilerne Thursday market started by Marius Fernandes. In the photo from left to right - Fr. Derrick Fernandes, Parish Priest of St. John The Baptist Church, Pilerne, Antoinette, Marius and Maria Goretti.

CHAPTER TWO

The Incredible Life of Antoinette

GOA-1930s- Growing Up

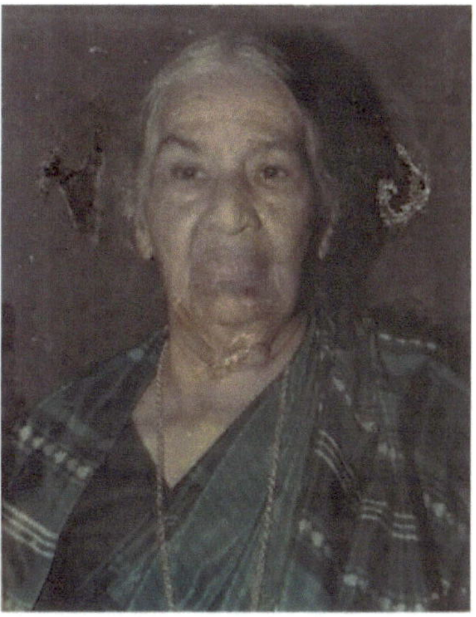

MX Fernandes and Maria Emilia Fernandes

Around 1930, the world was facing significant threats from fascism in Europe and dealing with the repercussions of the Wall Street Crash of 1929. In India, the liberation movement was gaining momentum and Goa was starting to feel the pressures of the Estado Novo under the Portuguese dictator Dr. Antonio Oliveira de Salazar. His dictatorial regime in Goa was marked by press censorship and restrictions on civil liberties.

Meanwhile, away from the politics of the time, in Malar, the D'Souzas rejoiced in the arrival of their baby girl on September 21, 1932, to Luis Mathias D'Souza and Arcanjela Piedade Rodrigues (Carolina). Her parents baptized her as Ana Regina Antoinette D'Souza. She was the youngest, after Lucy Verodiana, Vincent, Christine Rosalina, Richard Joaquim Joao and Bertha.

Little is known about her father, Luis Matias D'souza, who has roots in Maddant, Piedade was born in Dabul, Mumbai. Bits of information reveal his work as a medical assistant on board a swift-moving British luxury cruise liner, the ill-fated Lusitania, headed for Liverpool from New York. German U-boats torpedoed the vessel in 1915, leading to the tragic loss of lives. Fortunately, Luis was one of the 767 survivors after spending four days adrift at sea. He returned to Bombay (now Mumbai) after his successful rescue.

Antoinette, in a talkative mood, reveals what happened to her father. "My paternal grandmother, Ana Joaquina D'Costa, would tell us how she traveled to Mumbai to bring him home."

New information reveals that Luis Matias could have served in the Royal Indian Naval Reserve as he received three wartimemedals: the War Medal 1939-1945, a bronze and a Pacific Star.

When Antoinette was five years old, her family moved from Divar to the lush, green pastures of Salvador do Mundo (Saloi), about 13 kilometers from Panjim. The vibrant fields to the west of the village are nourished by the tidal creek that flows into the Mapusa River. During the monsoon season, the water bodies in the low-lying areas create a stunning landscape. The hilly regions are rich in teak, cashew and mango trees.

The determined and hardworking Ana Joaquina purchased a plot of land near the Saviour of the World Church cemetery for Rs.

200. "The 2,000-square-meter property didn't have a house. Neighbors helped gather the stones from a nearby quarry for construction," Antoinette recalls. Construction stopped midway since they ran short of stones to complete the rest of the house. Despite its unfinished state, the three-room stone has sheltered eight family members and had a large yard. The house remains the same to this day.

Antoinette's memories of the 1940s traverse a picturesque village landscape surrounded by her loved ones. Since there was no modern electricity, natural ventilation flowed through the home and *lampiãos* and candles provided warm illumination.

In pre-liberation Goa, the Portuguese presence was felt with the soldiers patrolling the village to keep a vigilant eye around. "The sight of them would scare the kids. They ran home after looking at the arms they carried with them," she recalls the *Gore, gore pit men,* referring to their white skin.

The devout Catholics attended mass next door at the Christ, the Saviour of the World Church, built in 1565. "A rose garden adorned the compound in those days. The well in the premises supplied water to the locals during shortages because of the perennial spring that ran below it," she says.

Education in pre-liberation Goa had limited options. The medium of instruction was Portuguese. Antoinette attended primary with a local schoolmaster, a man she recalls as 'Matreaguer' in Badem, a few kilometers from home. They walked the entire distance since there were no other means to commute.

"He was nearly 80 years old and had only a few students," she reveals the reason behind the name. She admits she wasn't particularly interested in academics and preferred being outdoors.

Her grandparents were devoted lovers of Konkani culture and aimed to instil the same passion in their grandchildren. They sent her and her sister Bertha to the Divine Providence school in Belgaum (today Belagavi), where Konkani was a subject. Their eldest sister, Christine, was already working at Primos Salon, Byculla, in Mumbai.

The journey to Belgaum was quite an adventure. As night fell over the village, the young girls and grandmother left home on foot to reach the canoe point. The small boat cut across the banks to reach Panjim in the dark.

The next day, they boarded a local bus (*caminhão*) from the main terminus in the city near the current Captain of Ports Jetty to Collem (Kulem), 62 kilometers in South Goa. They disembarked at Castle Rock station at the border. School agents there guided the Goan students to Belgaum.

Marius visits his mother's old school

Antoinette and Bertha studied at the school in Tilakwadi under the Canossian Daughters of Charity for the next four years. Coincidently, after marriage, Antoinette encountered the same order in Laare, Africa. Their father visited occasionally, carrying chocolates for them and the nuns.

Home for the summer holidays meant a *mudança* (change) by the shore. Families typically set off to the pristine, virgin beaches of Calangute or Baga, unlike the overcrowded eyesores of today. "We spent one or two weeks at Calangute Beach bathing in the sea and enjoying the fresh summer air. The beach was empty and very clean. We rented a hut *(khopti),* and the owners provided utensils for cooking. Those were simple pleasures, but we had a lot of fun," she recalls.

After schooling, Antoinette returned home to her grandmother and parents. By then, the rest of her elder siblings were married abroad. Carolina went off to Rhodesia (now Zimbabwe). Her brother Richard, who studied at St Joseph High School in Arpora, left for Zimbabwe.

Carolina helped Richard secure his first job. He later worked for the Mercantile Bank in Malawi. After Bertha moved to Lahore, it took her decades to be reunited with her sister Antoinette due to the Partition. Communication was difficult and one waited for months to receive a letter.

Life was simple in Goa. The young girl grew up surrounded by verdant hillsand an active community life. The family vegetable patch alongside the house had numerous fruit trees. Seasonal blooms like roses *(rosam),* dahlias and *shivtim* added color to the garden. In the summer, she savored the wild berries like *kanta, chunna* and *zamblam.*

The family reared pigs on the large property, with chickens for eggs and goats for milk. "We ate vegetables like *tidki midki, ragi* and lady fingers *(bhende)* from our patch. Our neighbors took us along to the fields and taught us how to grow," she reminisces.

Since her mother hardly involved herself with the housework, Antoinette gravitated to her grandmother, her pillar of strength for guidance. "My granny worked the entire day for the family and still found time to help the neighbors in their time of need. I owe all my knowledge to her," remembering her idol warmly.

Watching her grandmother's selfless work at close range left an imprint on the young girl. Decades later, she carried it across her travels. "We meet so many people who mum has helped. We are surprised because she never discussed it with us," shares Genevieve, one of her daughters, who visits Goa often from the UK.

Antoinette grew into a self-sufficient young woman, well-versed in cooking and managing the home. She spent her summers on the Saloi hills, cashew picking and plucking mangoes. "I used to carry baskets of cashews to the distiller to extract Niro on my way back."

She talks about the old process of *feni* extraction. "We walked into a large carved stone, tall enough to stand in. It had an outlet for the extracted liquid to flow out. We crushed the cashew apples with our bare feet, allowing the juice to flow through the hole. The dirt particles would escape, while the distilled juice trickled out drop by drop."

Would they wash their feet? "There was no need to wash our feet, as the dirt would flow out," she chuckles.

The duo roasted the nuts using hay to send parcels to her siblings abroad.

Young marriageable girls at 19 were sent for tailoring classes. She enrolled in Professor Amelia Tavares's classes to learn stitching and embroidery. Getting there wasn't easy. No local transportation meant walking 8 km daily from her home to Dos Waddo, Socorro.

"I left in the morning and returned in the evening. I would carry my lunch with me. Her classes ran full as her students came from Saloi, Maina and Porvorim," she recalls.

She didn't shy away from actively participating in parish activities. The former President of *Acção Catholique*, a lay group for women in Catholic Action, visited and cared for the sick, preparing meals, buying medicines, and praying with them. They also organized funeral arrangements for the poor—washing and dressing the deceased and getting flowers for their final journey.

She still recollects the old hymns she sang in the choir. Midway through the conversation, she joyfully breaks into *Sweetheart of Jesus*.

Antoinette's inherent love for music flows from her parents. "They were often invited to sing at weddings, which was a custom in those days," she recalls. "If the bride came from distant villages like Chorão, Aldona, or Bastora, she stayed the night with us. We would organize her *roce* ceremony the next morning. The neighbors helped cook and get the bride ready."

The songbird found her way to participate in the local *tiatr* (Konkani theatre) during village feasts. She broke societal barriers by taking on male roles as women were prohibited on stage.

She vividly recollects dressing up as a beggar, donning baggy clothes for authenticity in The *Prodigal Son*. She worked alongside the renowned music director, choirmaster, and composer Amiano D'Souza.

Antoinette loved watching the *tiatrs* of the famed H. Briton. "There was a play for every feast," she reminisces. "We would walk nearly four kilometers from home to Britona's village to watch his dramas. It would finish at midnight; we never missed it."

As she reached her 20s, it was time for Antoinette to find a suitable match. "I didn't like most of them," she laughs. "My sister Carolina warned me to accept the next proposal."

That's when Bernard Fernandes from East Africa arrived on the island. Bernard belonged to the pioneering MX Fernandes family from Kenya, who established one of the first Western-style bakeries in Eldoret.

The young Kenyan sought the help of a local matchmaker, Mathias 'Moti' Menezes. Moti, who knew of a *Divadkar* family in Salvador do Mundo, led him to Antoinette's home. They took a *vhoddem* (canoe) from São Mathias through Chorao to Saloi.

"I was the last girl he met," Antoinette chuckles. "He didn't like the ones before me." She had stepped out to buy sodas, when 'he was inside the house when I reached the gate. That was the first time he saw me.'

And so, the last wedding in the family was set. Moti took charge of the arrangements, from booking the hall to organizing the church ceremony. Unlike today's grand affairs, the wedding was simple: a church nuptial followed by a modest reception.

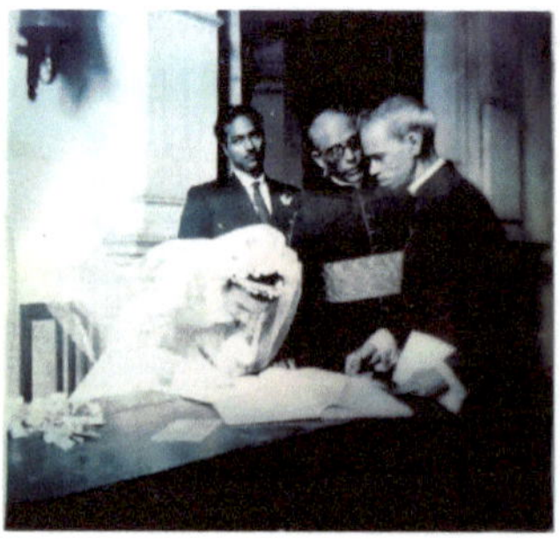

Mr. & Mrs. Mathias Xavier Fernandes
request the pleasure of the company of
Mrs. _________________________ & fly.
to witness the nuptials of their son

BERNARDINO   ANTHONITA

(daughter of Mr. & Mrs. L. M. D'Souza of Salvador do Mundo)
at the Convent of Dom Jesus, Velha Goa, on Saturday 3rd. May
1958, at 10 a. m. and thereafter to a reception
in the Hall of Dom Jesus.

S. Mathias, 24/4/58.

Antoinette and Bernard say - "I Do"

On May 3, 1958, Antoinette exchanged vows with Bernard at the Basilica de Bom Jesus in Old Goa. Wedding photos capture the young couple—the bride in a white gown stitched by the women in her village, surrounded by loved ones celebrating their union in a hall next to the Basilica.

What stands out is Antoinette's journey to the church that day. Her eyes, like an old projector reel, replay the moment from the day, every detail crystal clear. With no richly decorated wedding cars available from Salvador-do-Mundo to Old Goa, she had only one option.

"I rode a *vhoddem* from Saloi to Old Goa, all dressed in my bridal attire!" she recalls.

And was she ready for a new life in Africa? Her answer was simple: "I was happy to go abroad.

Kenya – 1960s

The warmth and comfort of Goan family life hadn't prepared Antoinette for the challenges awaiting her in the barren African wilderness. From the festive celebrations, parish activities, and carefree summer days spent in the hills, Laare, a remote settlement in Kenya, would become a training ground for survival.

The newly married couple eagerly anticipated their new life in the African bush. Antoinette carefully packed her trunk with essentials from Goa, including dried chilies, cashew seeds, coconut oil, and an array of spices—ingredients that would allow her to preserve the flavors of home in a foreign land. The lessons and memories from her upbringing in Goa would serve her well in the coming years.

A few weeks after their wedding, the couple embarked on their journey sometime in June. The canoe from Divar took them to the Old Goa bank, where a *caminhão* awaited passengers to take them to the capital, Panjim. Another bus took them to Mormugao port, where they boarded a steamer bound for Mombasa. Antoinette, 21, was excited for her maiden sea voyage and the new life ahead.

They arrived in Africa after atiring 12-day voyage. John Maciel and Gasper Viegas—coincidentally from Salvador-do-Mundo received them warmly at the port. The couple stayed briefly with Bernard's brother, late John, in Mombasa before continuing their journey to Laare, nearly 700 kilometers away in the Meru district.

Laare, located in a valley, was a remote and sparsely populated settlement with few Indians. The town's modest market square featured a row of tin-roofed shops. Bernard's family, the renowned MX Fernandes, established a bakery and provision store that also served as their home. Their Goan roots helped them introduce coffee, tea, cakes, and biscuits, making their shop a unique presence in the area.

The Fernandes bakery in Eldoret previously catered to European government officials, including provincial and district commissioners and Goan civil servants stationed in remote regions like Isiolo, Marsabit, Moyale, Wajir, and Mandera. Given their knowledge of baking and serving tea and coffee, the store drew celebrity visitors like Clark Gable, Ava Gardner, and Grace Kelly while they filmed the 1953 movie *Mogambo*.

Mervyn Maciel, a distinguished Goan in Kenya, recounted his experience meeting the Fernandes family in his book *Bwana Karani*: "We were newly married, and my wife looked happy to be there, at the home of the pioneering Goan family, Mr. and Mrs. MX Fernandes. They ran an efficient general store, which became a gathering place for Goans. It was here that the great *Born Free* films were made."

A modern structure stands where the Fernandes bakery once stood.

The shop was a vital hub for the local community. Bernard stocked groceries, petrol, and household supplies in one section while Antoinette baked cakes, biscuits, and bread—novelties for the local African population, who had little exposure to European cuisine.

The enterprising lady established a small tailoring enterprise. Setting up a tailoring business in such an isolated place was difficult. Luckily, since her brother-in-law, the late John, occupied a highly placed job with the UN, Antoinette sourced fabric, threads, and buttons from Mombasa and Nairobi. Her dresses caught the attention of the local ladies who lined up to purchase her designs.

Work began after breakfast at 10 a.m. The BBC World Service playing throughout the day, carrying news from across the globe. Some occasions, like England's World Cup victory in 1966, brought joy to the Goan family, who had football running in their veins.

Antoinette's ability to speak multiple languages—English, Konkani, and Hindi—and her grasp of Swahili enabled her to form friendships with Ethiopians and Somalis. "Since I worked at the store, I interacted with local Kenyans. My husband already knew the language, having been born there," she recalls.

Antoinette managed a family, and business and raised five children. The young mother gave birth to her eldest, Marius, in 1959 and within a decade, had four children in Africa, including the late Edgar (1961), Genevieve (1962), Maria Goretti (1964), and Fatima Bertha (1966).

There were no schools in the area. Antoinette home-schooled her children around the kitchen table or at her sewing machine. Marius vividly remembers the first song his mother sang to him: *Undir Mojea Mama*. It was through these songs and stories that he first learned about Goa.

Marius and his siblings grew up on a healthy dose of fresh produce, poultry and fruits.

Maria Emilia, took charge of the household after her husband MX returned to Goa and cooked their meals. Spices came in from nearby towns,and the kitchen carried the enticing aromas of Goan home-ground masalas.

Grace before meals, followed by the rosary at 8:30 p.m, was part of their daily schedule.

The Fernandes family were likely the first Catholics in the village, soon followed by other members. They attended Sunday mass two miles away at a church run by the Canossian nuns. Initially, mass was conducted in Latin or English, but it later switched to Swahili. Antoinette's strong devotion led her to start a donation drive at her shop to help build a permanent church structure, replacing the old makeshift tin hall. A new modern sprawling structure today stands in its place, shares Marius, who visited their old hometown on a visit.

The only Catholic feasts commemorated in the small community were Christmas and the Feast of St Francis Xavier on 3 December. The family prayed to St Francis on his feast day, followed by singing the famous *San Franciscu Xaviera* in Konkani.

Christmas brought out the true Goan spirit. Midnight Mass was followed by a festive lunch the next day, with cakes and biscuits baked over an open fire. Without modern ovens, Antoinette improvised by placing a smaller utensil inside a larger one over live coals. The Christmas spread included *batica*, *bolinhas* and *doce*.

During the holidays, the family made trips to Bernard's brother, the late John Fernandes, in Meru. On one occasion, Marius recalls attending an athletics tournament with a great Goan in the relay race. "I remember it was a large open field. There were no stadiums like the ones we have today. We sat on the grass eagerly waiting to catch the great Seraphino Ant in action. This was the first time I heard of him. When I returned to Laare recently, I visited his grave." Seraphino, originally from Chandor village in South Goa, was the first Kenyan athlete to win a gold at an international level. He won two events at the 1962 Commonwealth Games.

Life in Laare became increasingly perilous. Bernard often visited neighboring villages in Somalia to replenish supplies. Encounters with wild animals and hostile tribes proved dangerous. Marius recalls a harrowing tale of his father's Land Rover turtled over from a rhino attack. Bernard's quick reflexes and expertise to fix his vehicle allowed him to manage a narrow escape.

The constant threat of the Mau Mau Uprising next door in Somalia, with rebel groups wreaking havoc at night, proved unnerving for the family. The residents were accustomed to the rebel groups prowling the village. They either ran into the bunkers or sought cover in the hills. The Fernandes' had their bunker below the kitchen ready to jump in at any moment of threat.

One terrifying night, gunshots rang out. Huddled in fear indoors, the family knelt before the cross in prayer. Miraculously, when the group reached their door, the commander outside ordered his men, "Don't fire at this house. Leave them." Bernard's kindness towards the travelers—some of whom unknowingly belonged to the rebel group—had saved them.

Life in Kenya

The increasing violence forced the family to leave Laare, seeking refuge in Kindaruma, where they set up shop again. However, the arid conditions and poverty were overwhelming. Marius recalls, "Locals would collect flies in their sacks because they had nothing to eat."

The constant turmoil took a toll on Antoinette. She longed for home, especially after receiving distressing news about her parents' declining health. With news of the SS *Haryana* sailing for Goa, she seized the opportunity to return with her children.

The ship, managed by the Shipping Corporation of India, was one of the few steamers transporting Goans back and forth. The vessel featured a large open upper and lower deck like a dormitory. There were no private cabins on board the steamer. Passengers would quickly spread out their mats to secure a spot for the journey. The upper deck was covered to protect travelers from the heat and rain.

The 15-day voyage was filled with excitement for the children. During a stopover in Seychelles, small canoes surrounded the ship, creatinga floating market of exotic fruits and other goods.

Passengers stocked on food for the remainder of the trip, and meals were cooked on board using individual stoves. "I remember Mum packing biscuits and vegetables since there was no cafeteria," recalls Marius.

Since the passengers were mostly Goans, life on board was a lively show of Konkani music.

Back to Goa

The young mother, pregnant with her sixth child and five children, touched Mormugão port in January 1968. They took a bus to Panjim and later a canoe from the Old Goa bank to Divar. The ferry service between the Ribandar dock and the island hadn't yet started. Riding a canoe for the first time was a thrilling adventure for the children.

After settling in, she gave birth to her youngest, Mathias, on the island with the help of Maria Emilia. Later, she enrolled the others at Our Lady of Divar High School, a local school, to help them stay rooted in the Goa culture. Prisca Fernandes, the former headmistress who taught the children, noted Antoinette's love for the mother tongue in *Goencho Festekar, Marius Fernandes.*

She writes, 'Mrs. Antoinette Fernandes is an unassuming, down-to-earth lady, extremely fond of Konkani, our mother tongue...the parents made it a point to teach it to them. '

In April of that year, the children experienced Easter in Goa for the first time. Unlike their church services in Laare, the Lenten services in Divar included an elaborate Lenten ritual including the Good Friday procession, followed by the midnight mass on Saturday. The group trooped down the dark village road to attend the Easter Vigil services.

Summer Holidays in Divar

Antoinette instilled her faith in her children. She ensured that all her children were well-versed in Konkani prayers. They completed their Holy Communion and Confirmation classes before leaving for the UK. The moment was captured with a customary portrait at a photo studio. "Mum took my later brother, Edgar, and I to Hollywood Studios to Panjim for a photograph," recalls Marius.

Summer holidays were spent with all the cousins in the house. "We had a big group of 8 with us," says Marius. "Our cousins in boarding schools around Goa joined us in Malar. We had great fun with sing-along sessions in Konkani and English, and learned some Hindi numbers from them."

Antoinette introduced her children to *tiatrs* in the village. They attended shows by the great directors of the past like the late Alfred Rose, later M Boyer, late C Alvares and late Jacinto Vaz.

Bonderam in the 70s

The youngsters in Malar eagerly awaited the village feasts like Bonderam, the traditional flag festival. The yearly event in August commemorates the old mock battles between the villages. In the old days, celebrations were simple.

"We would congregate at the church with the flag bearers and follow them around the village. It was a pure local celebration. It took a week to prepare our *fotash*. We hunted for hollow bamboo, fill our pockets with *assalea*", recalls Marius. These early fests inspired the *festam* to come.

The festival over the years evolved to include a traditional float parade. Marius in recent years introduced a traditional *pasoi* in the evening to take visitors on an educational walk around Malar filled with music, dance, street plays, and food. Locals greet the guests with traditional sweets and share stories from the old.

Christmas in Divar back then was a grand affair. Preparations began from the first of December with the children starting work on the crib followed by the elder women making the traditional sweets. The family walked through the chilly winter night to attend midnight services on Christmas Eve. After mass, everyone met at the Malar Sports Club for the dance that wound up at 6 AM. The following morning brought a house full of the extended family for a Christmas lunch. Thus, the children spent their childhood amid family, developing a deep-rooted love for Konkani and Goan culture.

Antoinette gracefully handled the upbringing of her children and the care of her parents in Salvdor-do-Mundo, never relenting to the pressure. She kept a watchful eye on her parents, making short visits home with cash for their sustenance.

The Indo-Pak war brought further troubles for the family with remittances trickling in. Antoinette relied on money her husband sent from abroad, which sometimes never arrived due to theft or loss in the mail.

"We had generous neighbors who helped us with rice, fruits and vegetables when we had no money," Antoinette recalls.

Amid her struggles, another tragedy struck. News reached her of her sister Lucy's passing away. She hired a taxi to take her children to the Salvador-do-Mundo church for the funeral. They reached it just before the burial at the ceremony.

Antoinette and the children at Mumbai Airport before they departed for the UK.

After six years in Goa, the family prepared for another chapter: reuniting with Bernard in the UK, ready to embark on a new life in Europe.

UK - Mid-70s

With their lives in Africa under constant threat, Bernard moved to the UK in 1969, searching for a new future for his family. The Goan community in the UK helped him settle in. Finding accommodation as a man of color was a challenge. Fortunately, due to his strong work record, his employer at Cornwall Components generously offered him a large four-bedroom house at 31 Gwendolyn Road, Leicester. With his home and employment secured, it was time to welcome his family in the UK.

The Fernandes family pose in front of their home on
13 Gwendolyn Road.

Antoinette and the children left the warm tropical weather of Goa to the hostile cold wintery UK. The family arrived at Heathrow Airport from Mumbai at 8 AM greeted by a chill gusty wind. "As we landed, Dad greeted us with jumpers and blankets since we were completely unprepared for the freezing weather. We were dressed in plain cotton clothes," recalls Marius.

They were among the few Indian families in their quiet English neighborhood. By the 70s, Leicester had become more culturally diverse, welcoming immigrants from all over the world.

Their new home, previously owned by a coal merchant, had a large hall, dining room, and three additional rooms. The family lived there from 1976 to 1999 before Marius and his family returned to Goa in 2000, followed by his parents a year later.

A modern structure stands where the
old shop once stood.

The first two years in the UK were spent adjusting to a new life. Once the children settled into their studies at St. Paul High School, she joined Corah, a premier hosiery company specializing in woollen imports.

Despite her demanding schedule, she balanced work and home seamlessly, starting her day at 6 AM and returning home by 8 PM. Sundays were dedicated to family. She used these moments to teach her children Konkani numbers, preserving their cultural roots.

Antoinette's dedication to her work did not go unnoticed. A Ghanaian businessman, M R Mensah recognising a hard and honest worker, approached her to manage the Leicester City Café near the King Power football stadium. She ran the café for two years, serving sandwiches, tea, coffee, and traditional English breakfast items to players and locals.

Amidst her busy life, she remained committed to her parents, securing them a senior home and sending money and food regularly. During her visits to Goa, she took them back to Divar for feast days, ensuring they remained connected to their heritage. They passed away peacefully in their 90s.

(Left) Antoinette and her family host the Alfred Rose group
and (Right) with the legend Alfred Rose

Antoinette's fluency in Konkani facilitated connections with Goans arriving in the UK from across the globe. This made her a sought-after figure. The Goa Overseas Association (GOA) in Leicester and the larger branch in Beckenham, Kent, sought her assistance with cultural events.

In 1980, she hosted the first Konkani *tiatr Konn Mozo Pai* at Sacred Heart Church Hall, involving her daughters in music and theatrical performances.

First Konkani Tiatr staged in Leicester, UK

Antoinette's deep understanding of tiatr facilitated the introduction of Alfred Rose, a legendary Konkani *tiatrist*. She also played a crucial role in introducing them to the UK Goan community.

Her persistent efforts and organizational skills ensured the troupe stage their play in front of a sell-out crowd in Harrow. She sought the assistance of her daughter Genevieve's connection to the Greater London Council.

After three months of persistent efforts, on March 9, 1986 the event was a resounding success.

Family friend and horticulturist Miguel Braganza praises her dedication to Konkani and her warm hospitality, a trait passed down to her children and grandchildren. "Whether in Africa or the UK, she maintained her *mãe bhas* (mother tongue), ensuring her family spoke Konkani fluently. Her granddaughter, Gemma, even delivered her *tiatr* dialogue in the correct dialect. That is commendable."

She was also a voracious reader, keeping up with Goan affairs through publications like Goa Today. She used her vast knowledge to educate the Goans in the Leicester area through her regular contributions to the *Goa Voice* by the Leicester Goan Association. Flipping through its pages reveals a surprising side of Antoinette where the writer-side of Antoinette is revealed. Writing in

Konkani with English translations, her favorite topics included Goa, song lyrics, and recipes.

In an introduction to Anna Fernandes, as she is referred too, the publication writes, 'I would like to introduce Anna Fernandes to those of you who are not familiar with her work in promoting the Goan Culture, and who in the past has taught Konkani to anyone and everyone who has been keen to learn.'

She writes about the havoc caused by the monsoons in Goa in an article. She observes the difference in weather as in the old days 'parents used to say, the rain either starts on the 5th or 15th of June. 5th of June is Mirg which is the Feast that the Hindus celebrate. The 13th of June as you know, is St Anthony's day...'

(Left) Save Goa stall at Scogo, UK (Right) Save Goa conference at House of Commons, UK with M.P. Keith Vaz

Environmental issues in Goa, such as Nylon 66 and the impact of tourism, spurred her to action. She launched the Save Goa Campaign, raising awareness among Goans in the UK, despite facing threats for her activism.

"Mum set up a stall at World Goa Day events to educate Goans in the UK about issues back home. People ridiculed us, and I even received threatening calls," Marius recalls. The campaign ran for five years, eventually joining forces with Roland Martins's GoaCan initiative in Goa.

Beyond language and culture, Antoinette engaged in community service, volunteering with the Scouts and Guides Movement in Leicester and participating in fundraisers and car boot sales.

Antoinette collection of articles in her scrapbook.

Antoinette's love for reading led to an unlikely hobby—scrapbooking news articles about the British royals, politics, and Goan affairs. One clipping chronicled actress Rita Hayworth's scandalous romance with Prince Aly Khan; another followed comedian Peter Sellers' life. When asked why she did it, she replied, "I want to look back and read it all one day. I learned this habit from my late son Edgar."

After Marius married late Sheela and had two children, Ashley and Gemma, the parents stayed with their son in Leicester. Her daughters had moved to London. Her grandchildren, Ashley and Gemma, grew up under their grandmother's loving eye, who nurtured them with Goan values and a love for Konkani. By the time Marius and family returned to Goa in 2000, they surprised everyone with their fluency of the language.

Retirement in Goa

Although Antoinette built a strong life in the UK, the cold weather left her yearning for the warmth of Goa. On her return in 2001 to Divar, she cared for the elders in her family including her husband and, later, her siblings, Christine, Bertha, and Richard.

Age may have caught up with her physically at 91 but not her spirit. Her slim face, wrinkled from experience, doesn't miss a chance to spread smiles or throw in a quick joke to lighten the conversations.

Most mornings, she's sipping her tea while reading the newspapers on the *soppo*. With silver-rimmed glasses perched on her nose, she reads the *Herald, Times of India, Navhind Times, The Goan,* and *Goa Samachar.*

"Our family, having traveled across three continents, relied on books and periodicals to stay informed. Reading has been a habit passed down through generations," she says.

She stayed in touch with friends and family in the UK. Her ties with the Church were instrumental in bringing a pilgrimage to Goa from the UK, organized by Fr. John Tavares. Born in Dar-es-Salaam, Tanzania, with roots in Raia and Salvador do Mundo, Fr. Tavares first met Antoinette in Leicester. Writing to Marius from the UK about his trips to Goa, he describes her as "a highly cultured lady who kept Goan traditions alive in England. I don't think she was appreciated by Goans as much as she should have been, yet she remained merciful and helpful to everyone."

During his first visit to Goa, he stayed with Antoinette, learning about Goan culture and folklore. Their discussions led to a pilgrimage from Market Harborough to Goa, staying at Jose Marino's Colonia Hotel in Varca and visiting holy sites. "Antoinette welcomed us in Divar, taking us on a walking tour before hosting a grand feast prepared by the islanders. With the bishop's consent, I celebrated Mass in Divar Church—an unforgettable experience for the locals and pilgrims alike."

Today, visits to her home on Divar Island are filled with lively discussions and recollections. During festivals like *Bonderam* and *Potekar*, she shares stories of old traditions. In a video interview, she demonstrates how fotash (bamboo pop guns) were used during Bonderam.

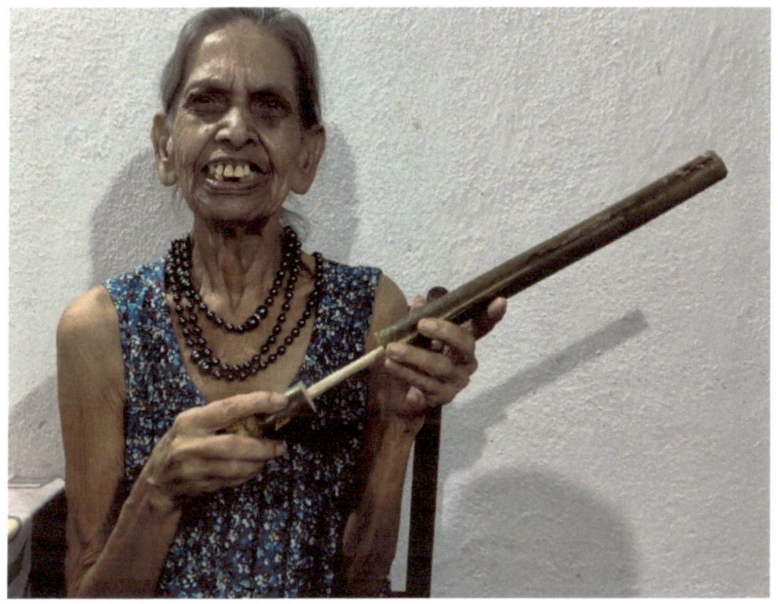

Fotash commonly used in Bonderam on Divar Island.

Yeh Assalea. (Pointing to the assalea leaves) Assalea, fotassin ghalun zai, ani...thoooo!!! koroon marun zai. (Demonstrates) Te Bonderacher marunk jay, punn bhurge lokacher marta. Ani te hatar boslyaar, haat zovta. Bonderam Divadech zata, Divadde ani Malara.

"These berries are called *Assalea.* We inserted them in the *Fotash,* a hollow bamboo stick, and fired them at flags—though mischievous boys often aimed at people instead, causing pain and irritation. *Bonderam* is celebrated in Divar and Malar."

She enjoys posing with *Potekar* (an age-old tradition of men dressed in shabby clothes) on her *balcão,* her words transporting visitors to the golden days of a beloved homeland.

(Left) Potekar Fest, Antoinette shares her memories with friends and (Right) Saying cheese with a Potekar

Her vivid memories played a key role in helping Marius revive many of Goa's forgotten traditions through his festivals. He says, "She's a great example of how you gain wisdom from every experience. I'm lucky to be her son. My mum is always willing to share her knowledge and encourages others to do the same."

Despite her advancing years and health challenges, Antoinette remains cheerful, extending warm hospitality to all who visit. In her stories lie the last threads of a Goa once rich in tradition and culture - a Goa now fading with time but forever alive in her memories.

CHAPTER THREE

'Our Hero' -Recollections of a loving mother and grandmother

'A Tribute to My Wonderful Mum' - Festacar Marius Fernandes

It has been a journey through the generations, celebrating 64 years of love, resilience and joy with my dear mum. She has been with me all my life, enriching it with experiences, love and the unwavering bond of family.

As the eldest son, I have been on a remarkable journey through time, traversing continents and witnessing the beauty of a life well-lived. Our story begins in the picturesque landscapes of Laare, Kenya, where I, the first of six children, took my first steps and learned the essence of family from the embrace of my parents - Bernard and Antoinette Fernandes.

Kenya - with its vibrant colors and diverse culture, imprinted in me a sense of belonging and an appreciation for the beauty of life. As we transitioned our lives to Leicester, United Kingdom, the vibrant tapestry of our family unfolded against the backdrop of new challenges and opportunities. The teenage years brought with them a blend of cultural influences as we adapted to the British way of life while holding onto the cherished traditions of our Kenyan and Goan heritage.

Through the ups and downs, it was the strength of family ties that guided us, shaping the values that define us today. After years of growth and exploration, destiny led me to Goa, where I found not just a new chapter but a home filled with warmth and love. Goa, with its sun-kissed beaches and the vibrant tapestry of its people, became the backdrop of my married life.

It was here that I, surrounded by the lush beauty of St. Mathias on Divar Island, planted the roots of my own family, cherishing the lessons passed down through generations.

Living a life that spans three continents is no small feat and the heart of this journey lies in the unwavering companionship between a mother and her eldest son. From the open plains of Kenya to the bustling streets of the UK and the serene landscapes of Goa, my mother's resilience and love have been my constant guides. It is a unique bond that has weathered the storms of time, embracing change while holding onto the core values that define us as a family.

As I reflect on the past 65 years, I am filled with gratitude for the myriad of experiences that have shaped our family. Each twist and turn, every joy and challenge, has contributed to the tapestry of our shared history. From the laughter that echoed through our home to the quiet moments of reflection, every chapter is a testament to the strength of family ties and the enduring spirit of Antoinette Fernandes.

If today I am known as Goencho Festacar, all the credit goes to my mum and her influence on me in my childhood days, telling us stories about Goa of the 1950s, teaching us Konkani in the UK and celebrating all cultural and religious festivals that let us rejoice and also revel in our heritage.

Since 1999 and our 100 festam, she has been my library, my internet and information bank and with our neighbors, all gathering in the Call center (Balcão) discussing the day's news and tomorrow's gossip. On my social media page, we have been sharing my mum's old Konkani songs and oral stories of the past. She is responsible for all the knowledge that I possess and shares with me everything about Goa and our unique way of life.

The story of the Fernandes family is a story of resilience, adaptability. Above all, a celebration of the enduring power of love. In the warm embrace of family and friends, surrounded by the echoes of a life well-lived, we toast to the matriarch who has been the heart and soul of our journey.

Dear Mum—may the years ahead be as vibrant and filled with love as the remarkable life you have lived.

'To An Incredible Mum' -*Genevieve*

Mum has always been an incredible mother—firm yet deeply respectful of her children. She set clear boundaries when it came to schoolwork and chores but balanced discipline with empathy. She truly listened to us, valued our perspectives and supported us in every phase of life.

Our life was simple, yet it was filled with laughter. Mum's sharp sense of humor could lighten any moment, and to this day, her quick wit keeps us entertained. Whether we are gathered around the dining table in Divar or sitting in the balcão, she never fails to crack a joke.

She juggled multiple roles with remarkable ease—working in a hospital, retail and even running a café. At times, she held three or four jobs at once. Looking back as a mother myself, I often wonder how she managed it all. She was up by 6 a.m, ensuring we were ready for school, our meals were prepared and our homework was done—all while handling her own demanding responsibilities.

Despite the challenges, I never saw her crumble under pressure. She never burdened us with her troubles, though I occasionally caught her lost in thought, perhaps searching for solutions. But no matter how tough things got, her faith kept her strong.

Prayer was and still is, an essential part of her life. That steadfastness has been passed down to us, and I've carried it forward with my own children. In the UK, she was an active member of the Konkani choir, recruiting all the youngsters—including me, despite my lack of singing skills. Konkani was close to her heart and she made sure we embraced it too. She taught us to sing in the language, gave us voice lessons before every performance and even choreographed our songs. As the event days approached, she prepared our costumes herself, drawing on her skills as a trained seamstress.

Mum also instilled in us a deep sense of empathy, especially toward the elderly and vulnerable. From a young age, she taught us the importance of kindness. I still remember how she would always give up her seat for seniors on the bus—something we continue to do as adults without a second thought.

Above all, Mum's love for life is infectious. She often reminds us, "It's not always about the money." After I started working, she would ask why I was pushing myself so hard. Now, with my children grown, I question whether I really needed to be so consumed by the 9-to-5 grind. Her words made me rethink my priorities. She valued hard work but never let go of life's lighter moments.

Mum's strength, wisdom and humor continue to shape us. And for that, we are endlessly grateful.

'Mum is Indestructible' -*Fatima Bertha & Maria Goretti*

Antoinette at home in Divar with her daughters Maria Goretti
(left) and Maria Fatima Bertha (right)

Fatima Bertha was just six months old when she returned to Divar. She fondly recalls her childhood spent with her siblings and mother on the island. With their father away in the UK for nearly a decade, her mother took on the dual role of both parents. "She did it all," Fatima remembers, seated next to her sister Maria Goretti, who adds, "We all thought she is indestructible." Both daughters are frequent visitors to their mum.

Fatima Bertha explains how their multi-tasking mum balanced all the roles easily. "She cooked, cleaned, helped with our studies and ensured we succeeded. I don't know how she managed it."

Days on the island were tough. "We had two rooms, and the bath was inside. The modko (a big earthen pot) had to be heated for hot water inside. We used to put one big mat for six of us to sleep." Despite the bleak struggle, Maria Goretti recalls only the happy days. "Dad would send the money in a brown paper envelope, and sometimes money went missing in the post, or he would get robbed. Mum used to wait for the money to feed us and pay for the school fees. But she kept us going. She never showed it."

Fatima Bertha also remembers her mother's warm and amicable nature with everyone she encountered. "Despite the tough times, she never had an argument with the neighbors," she says.

Her mother played a pivotal role in shaping her children's upbringing, instilling strong moral values and manners rooted in her deep faith. "She made sure we said our prayers before every meal, a practice we still follow today. The old-fashioned Goan manners are still with us, and she still gives us a gentle reprimand if we forget," Fatima Bertha chuckles.

Their mother's love for Konkani and the language was passed down to her children. Two weeks before leaving for the UK, their grandfather, Luis Mathias, taught them songs like Undir Mojea Mama and Tamde Rosa and their mother continued to teach them more once they settled in England.

"I still remember the day we arrived in the UK on January 3, 1976. The first thing our parents told us was that from that day forward, no one was allowed to speak English at home. That's why we still remember Konkani," Fatima Bertha recalls. "Mum taught the local kids Konkani. She kept the language going for many people and joined the Leicester Goan Association. She ensured proper Goan meals were made on Sundays," Maria Goretti recalls.

Hearing her daughter recount these memories, Antoinette adds, "I wanted them to speak Konkani at home so they wouldn't forget our language and they could use English outside."

Music was a constant presence in their lives. After Sunday mass, as the family gathered to do the chores, Antoinette would sit with her children and sing cantaram around the table as the meal was being prepared.

"She would make us sing at every Goan event. Sometimes I liked it and as children, it was a little embarrassing," confesses Maria Goretti.

The Grandchildren

'A Tribute to Granny Antoinette Fernandes' - Ashley Fernandes

My earliest recollections of my granny, Antoinette Fernandes, are set in Leicester, UK, where she lived with my late grandfather, Bernard Fernandes. Born at the Royal Infirmary, Leicester, I was surrounded by the love and warmth of my family from the very beginning. My grandmother suggested that both my grandfathers' names be included when I was baptized at Sacred Heart Church, Leicester. Thus, my name - Ashley Luis Mathias Fernandes. My first name, Ashley, was chosen by my father, Marius Fernandes, a devoted Leicester City supporter, after the club's star striker, Ashley Ward.

As the firstborn, I spent much of my early years at my grandparents' lovely house on Gwendolyn Road, Leicester, while my parents, Marius and the late Sheela Fernandes, were at work. My grandparents' home was a sanctuary where I felt cherished and safe. They filled my days with joy, often watching TV with me and sharing their love for music, especially Konkani songs. Despite living in the UK, my grandparents were staunch supporters of the Konkani language and culture. Konkani was the language of our household and through it, I connected deeply with my heritage.

My grandparents were not only my caretakers but also my first teachers. They enrolled me at Sacred Heart Primary School and took on the responsibility of dropping me off and picking me up each day. Their dedication to my education and well-being was evident in every aspect of their lives. They instilled in me the values of hard work, respect and the importance of family.

In 1999, my parents decided to move to St. Mathias, Divar Island, in Goa. Shortly, my grandparents shifted to Goa as well. The transition to Goa was made smoother by my grandmother, who spoke Konkani fluently and helped me settle into the new environment. I was enrolled in Our Lady of Divar High School and began participating in local activities, thanks to her support.

My father, Marius, was active in the Parents and Teachers Association and played a significant role in bringing the renowned Pilar Music School to the island. This opportunity marked the beginning of my formal music education. I began learning the keyboard, solfeggio and guitar with my granny's constant encouragement and guidance. Recognizing my growing interest in music, my grandmother bought me a very expensive saxophone made in France, a treasured possession to this day. She attended many of my shows around Goa, cheering me on with pride and joy.

With my father's help, I formed the Sunshine Children's Band and we performed at various events across Goa. My grandmother was always present, supporting me and sharing in my achievements. Her unwavering belief in my abilities fueled my passion for music and motivated me to pursue my dreams.

When I attained my music degree at the SAE College of Music in London, my grandmother was there to witness one of the proudest moments of my life. Her presence at my graduation was a testament to the incredible journey we had shared and the countless sacrifices she had made for our family.

Granny has been my greatest supporter, my mentor and my inspiration. Her love, wisdom and encouragement has shaped who I am today. This tribute is a celebration of her remarkable life and the indelible impact she has had on our family. I am immensely grateful for the opportunity to document her amazing journey and contribute to preserving her legacy.

As we look back on the moments that defined our lives, we are reminded of the enduring bond that ties us together. Granny's life is a testament to the power of love, resilience and unwavering support. Through this tribute, I hope to honor her memory and share the stories that have shaped our family's history.

'Cherishing the Bonds of Generations: My Journey with Granny Antoinette' -Gemma Fernandes

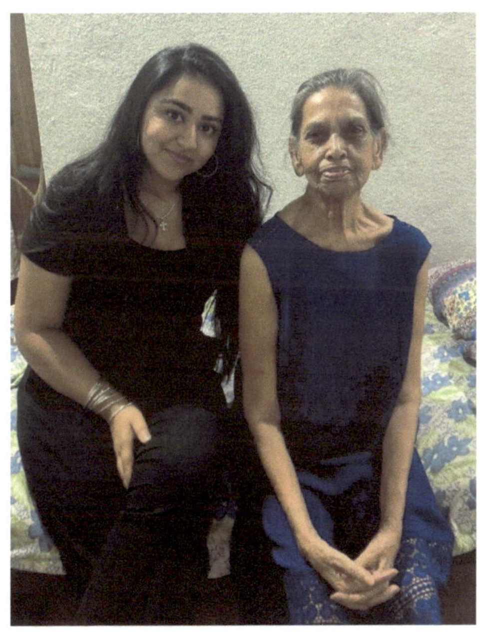

In the bustling city of Leicester, UK, my earliest memories find their roots in the warmth of my grandparents' home. Antoinette and Bernard Fernandes, my loving grandparents, opened their doors and hearts to me from the moment I could toddle around. While my parents Marius Fernandes and late mum Sheela Fernandes toiled away at work, it was in their cozy abode that I found solace and a second home.

Despite being thousands of miles away from our ancestral land of Goa, my grandparents were unwavering advocates of our Konkani heritage. Inside their home, the melodious tunes of Konkani songs filled the air, and the comforting cadence of the

Konkani language was a constant presence. It was here, nestled in the heart of the UK, that I imbibed the essence of my culture, thanks to their steadfast commitment.

In 1999, as my parents charted a new course back to our roots on Divar Island, Goa, my grandparents swiftly followed suit. The transition was seamless, as if the Goa they had left behind years ago had been patiently waiting for their return. Our family unit, now reunited on Goan soil, flourished amidst the lush greenery and tranquil waters of Divar Island.

As I enrolled in Our Lady of Divar High School and began to immerse myself in local activities, my grandmother's presence became my guiding light. Her fluency in Konkani proved to be invaluable, smoothing my path as I ventured into the world of Konkani tiatr. With each performance, her eyes sparkled with pride, her applause a symphony of unwavering support.

Through the years, as I traversed the winding paths of adolescence and beyond, my grandmother remained my steadfast companion. Her unwavering belief in me, her encouragement and her presence at every milestone filled me with a sense of purpose and belonging.

Today, as I embark on the journey of documenting her remarkable life, I am filled with gratitude for the opportunity to immortalize her legacy. In every word penned, in every memory shared, I hope to honor the bond we share—a bond that transcends time and space, weaving together the threads of generations past, present and future.

Granny Antoinette, with your love as my compass, I navigate life's ever-changing landscape with confidence and grace. Thank you for being my greatest supporter, my guiding light and my eternal source of love.

CHAPTER FOUR

Notes from Friends

ALEXYZ

One sun shiny dawn,
A Monarch Butterfly Bernardo
Braves the win and waves
Across Mandovi descends
Like a lost prodigal bro.
On the emerald island of Divar
He flutters and flirts
Alluring Ana attracts

His baffled eyeballs
Besotts a shy gal
And even her folks
With Swahili jokes.
They fly high to Kenya
Like the Resurrection, they ascend
Their love clouds blowing
Higher than the Kilimanjaro
Two hat-tricks
Six siblings in a row.
In 1975 sang their last
Malaika in Africa land
Conquering the Conquerors
Build their nest
In Leicester England.
Anna's love affairs
Across continents
Never dented her intense
Phobia for Goa since young
Embedded in her Mother's tongue.
A flag bearer of Konkani
In Africa and UK
Is now noted indelibly
In the Goa files.
She even escorted
The tongues
Ambassador Alfred Rose
To the British Isles.
Infatuated as she was
With Goa and Konkani
At 92 Anna Fernandes
Acclaimed by all
The nonagenarian from
St Mathias in Divar stands tall.
A living monument

Of all things Goan
An authentic Niz Goenkar
In whose shadow
Strides strong and steady
Her torch bearer
Marius Fernandes
Goencho Festacar.

"Antoinetta Fernandes, This is your life" -Steve White

You are, in my estimation, one of the greatest Goans and I thank you for always making me welcome when over there.

How interesting that our lives overlap in the way they do.

In your time spent living in Leicester, UK you worked as a tea lady at the Moat School, where 20+ years before, I was a very young, impressionable pupil.

Then you popped up at my local Leicester City Cafe opposite the Leicester Tigers serving fresh sandwiches, teas, and coffees. Not just serving the community but some of the LCFC players who dropped in regularly!

I distinctly remember on my second trip to Goa with my family how you made us all so welcome. In no time we felt at home. I returned to Goa and particularly the Island of Divar because you epitomized the best of Goa.

You and your family have a lovely way of learning about life through the prism of Goa.

I would love to be with you on your big day but as you will understand there are duties to be attended to in Leicester where I still happily reside.

One last little thought Antoinetta why don't we share a little more what we both and our families have living in phenomenal places like Goa and Leicester -just a thought.

'Antoinette's Story Requires a Netflix Series'
-George Goodchild

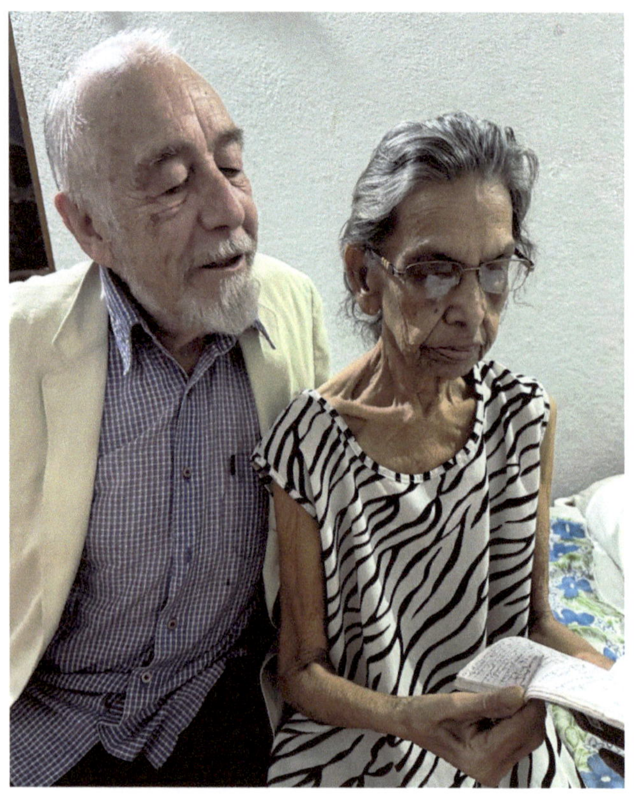

Antoinetta Regina Anna Fernandes has a long and complex story that requires a book and a Netflix series. Here are some things I think I know. In 1967, she and her husband, Bernard, were forced to abandon their home and their business in Kenya because of unrest and violence. The wind of change was whipping up across the continent of Africa. Anna and five children, with another on the way, set sail for Goa, arriving at Margao and then on to Divar Island.

Bernard went to England, where he began working 24/7 to buy a house for his growing family. After some years of hardship, Anna and six children went to join him in Leicester, where the children finished their education, having already received good foundations on Divar.

Twenty years later, my wife, Kathy, and I met the eldest of those Fernandes children in Panaji. It was Mario and his wife, Sheela. They were also on holiday and invited us to visit them in Divar. It was the day of the festival of Potekar, when, for some reason, the grown-ups, wearing scary masks, are encouraged to frighten the children. Frightening kids always seems a good idea to me. It was then that we met Anna, who was again living back on the island. Over the years, Kathy and I have come to know the Fernandes family and their friends. All are special but the most special is Anna. She never fails to tell me that it's good to say 'hello' to me again and even better to say 'goodbye'. She thinks that's funny- I think it's just plain rude – O.K, it's a bit funny, I suppose.

Recalling Our Encounter -Mervyn Maciel

Although Antoinette is three years younger than I am, she has a photographic memory and remembers many events from her childhood.

I first met Antoinette many years ago (can't remember the precise year) but it must have been in the seventies.

Being a lover of Konkani and Goan music, song, dance and theatre, I was attending a concert in North London where some prominent Goans, notably Alfred Rose, would be performing.

It was a lovely evening, and the hall was packed to capacity. I can't now recall the theme of the tiatr but was over the moon to hear many Konkani numbers.

It was here that I met Antoinette very briefly as it was quite late when the concert was over, and we had a Tube and train to catch for the return journey home in Surrey.

During that brief encounter, Antoinette, introduced herself, telling me how she knew my whole family singling out my dad's younger brother, Uncle Luis – the noisy one in the Family! Uncle Luis was well known not just in our Vaddo, but in the whole village. He had a thunderous voice and could frighten young children. Antoinette knew my grandmother well and our adopted African maid, Marie, from Mozambique who was part of our family.

He used to get up to all sorts of mischief, tease young village women and girls and generally make a nuisance of himself. He had an imposing personality and as he had a fair complexion, he could well be mistaken for an Italian!

The other villager Antoinette remembered was my immediate neighbour in Goa – the late Gaspar Viegas a very close friend from Goa days and later in Kenya and London.

This is all I can remember of Antoinette, while also speaking briefly to her by phone (thanks to modern technology), when Marius, his daughter and two sisters were visiting me here in England to record a video of my own recollections of their wonderful grandparents – my good friends – the late Mr. & Mrs. M.X.(affectionately known as 'Moti') Fernandes of Isiolo.

It is on this occasion that Antoinette sang familiar Konkani songs! A day to remember.

Viva! (as my Uncle Luis would always say)

An Exceptional Lady - *Tony Fernandes*

Antoinetta has had an extraordinary life. She went to Kenya in 1958, plucked from a quiet Goan village and thrust literally into the wilds of Kenya. Laré, where she spent her first few years, was a semi-arid land and very basic with no running water or electricity or hospitals and where law & order was like in the Wild West. Somali brigands often raided the area, and making a living here clearly required more than faith, guts, courage, resilience, and hard work.

Bringing up children without losing any in a region of very high child mortality is another testament to both good care and good luck. In the early sixties, the family moved to Kindaruma on the banks of the Tana River where a big dam was being built. Moving to a newly created town in the middle of nowhere and through their shop serving workers and their families while bringing up five children under ten was no mean feat.

In 1967, while Bernard stayed in Kenya Antoinetta returned to Goa where Mathias was born. The difficulties of bringing up six children during this time in Malar together with granny can only be imagined particularly when looked at through today's lens.

Packing up again to join Bernard and start a new life in freezing England in the mid-seventies was yet another well-managed major disruption. Life in England wasn't easy. When the children grew up and left home to live independent lives, their job of parenting was done. However, before they could finally return to Malar to retire, they and all of us tragically lost our beloved Edgar - a pain which lingers on.

Unlike most people Antoinetta has had in effect many lives - Goa, Kenya, Goa, UK and Goa again encompassing very different cultures, climates and times. Life in the 1950s and the 2020s is like living on different planets. My Mum, Bertila who shares a somewhat parallel life tells me that Antoinetta is truly exceptional and to be admired.

She says Antoinetta is always calm, grounded, modest, simple and inherently cheerful. She encapsulates all this and more into 92 years of a remarkable life.

A Tribute to Mario's Remarkable Mother -Douglas Fernandes, London, UK

To the woman whose warmth and hospitality left an indelible mark on my heart. As we celebrate your 92nd birthday, I am filled with gratitude for the friendship and love you've shared with us. Your kindness, wisdom, and unwavering support have touched our lives in profound ways.

When I first met you during my student days in South Shields, little did I know that our encounter would blossom into a lifelong connection. Your home became a sanctuary—a place where laughter echoed, stories flowed, and memories were etched into our souls.

Leicester, UK, witnessed your family's unwavering commitment to preserving Goan heritage. You dreamed of returning to our roots, and your son Mario, whom I consider a dear friend, carried that dream forward. Together, you supported your son to recreate forgotten festivals, breathed life into traditions, and kept the flame of our culture burning.

Your involvement, dear mother, is etched in every memory Mario shares on his blogs on social media like FB and Instagram. Nostalgia dances in your eyes as you remind him of days gone with traditional songs in Konkani, English, and Swahali, reminiscing the fragrant spices of Goa, the monsoon rains, and the laughter that echoed through your home.

As a family, we owe you immeasurable gratitude. Your open arms welcomed me during my young college days, offering advice and warmth and family love when I spent long periods away from my family. You taught us that family extends beyond blood, embracing kindred spirits across continents.

Dear Aunt Antoinette, a loving soul, kindest person and keeper of memories, may your health remain steadfast, and may the echoes of our shared past continue to resonate.

CHAPTER FIVE

Sing Along

Harambee Harambee

> *"This is one of my favorite songs that I sing and encourage others to join in. Here we go! " - Antoinette*

Kenyan classic *Harambee Harambee,* released in the early 1970s, reflects the aspirations of postcolonial Kenya to rebuild their nation together, sung by the legendary Daudi Kabaka (1939-2001).

Harambee harambee tuimbe pamoja
Harambe harambee tuimbe pamoja
Harambee harambee tuimbe pamoja
Tujenge serikali
Wengi walisema kenya itakuwa matata
Watu wote wastaarabu
Wananchi harambee tuvute pamoja
Muongoze na usalama
Watu wa kenya hatuna ubaguzi.
Kila rangi tunaipenda

Razachem Jevonn

"This is my most favorite hymn, it talks about fest and being Inclusive. Jesus teaches us and my son practices Jesus' teachings through his curated festam" - Antoinette.

Sorginchea razan kele,
Jevonn vhodlea festachem,
Razkunvrachea lognachem (X2)
Angostram ghalun novim,
Razachea jevnak soglim,
Bosum-ia dhadosponnim.
Amontronn sogleank dhadlam,
Ontor koslich korunkna,
Tor hadun Naka niba,
Razkuvor put Devacho,
Monxam'soiman ailolo,
Jezu tarok monxancho.
Rup tachem sundor sobit,
Mukhu tachem loklokit,
Angavlim bhi dhomdomit.

Dhalia

Tuka polloun Dalia murgottalim
Athan dovrun tuka poxetalim (X2)
    Ch.:
Fulam bhitor sobit tunch re Dahlia
Dekhun tujea mogan poddlam Lilia
Tujea vinnem sukhuch naim re mhaka
Vegim korun ghe tuji marida....Repeat
    Sodanch donprachea bara vorar
Yeun ubem ravo tum zonelar
    Suriacho uzvadd poddtoch tuje samkear
Sarkem assa distalem sorgar (X2)
    Ch.:
Fulam bhitor sobit tunch re Dahlia
Dekhun tujea mogan poddlam Lilia
Tujea vinnem sukhuch naim re mhaka
Vegim korun ghe tuji marida....Repeat
    Adeus ghara anv vetam
Nimanno abras tuka ditam
    Zori tori mannka sandxi zalear maka
Vortantulim soglim astelim tuka (X2)
    Ch.
Fulam bhitor sobit tunch re Dahlia
Dekhun tujea mogan poddlam Lilia
Tujea vinnem sukhuch naim re mhaka
Vegim korun ghe tuji marida....Repeat
    Vegim korun ghe tuji marida
    Vegim korun ghe tuji marida

Daisy, Daisy

"We used to sing this commonly for gatherings, while cooking, gardening, etc. I sang it to my children and my children are all well-placed in life today. It gives me contentment." - Antoinette.

There is a flower within my heart
Daisy, Daisy
Planted one day by a glancing dart
Planted by Daisy Bell
Whether she loves me or loves me not
Sometimes, it's hard to tell
Lovers quite willing to share the lot
And share it with Daisy Bell
Daisy, Daisy,
Give me your answer, do!
I'm half crazy,
All for the love of you!
It won't be a stylish marriage,
I can't afford a carriage,
But you'll look sweet on the seat
Of a bicycle built for two!
We will go tandem as man and wife
Daisy, Daisy
Wheeling the way down the road of life
I and my Daisy Bell
When the night's dark, we can both despise
Policemen and lamps as well
Love is quite willing to share the lot
And share it with Daisy Bell
Daisy, Daisy,
Give me your answer, do!

I'm half crazy,
All for the love of you!
It won't be a stylish marriage,
I can't afford a carriage,
But you'll look sweet on the seat
Of a bicycle built for two!

CHAPTER SIX

Recipes

Ugali

It is like porridge but denser and made from white maize meal or maize flour and enjoyed with a gravy dish or vegetables. It is the staple diet of the indigenous people of Kenya.

Ingredients

1. cup maize/corn
2. cups room temperature water

Instructions

- Heat water over a medium heat in a deep pan with a handle.
- Sprinkle about 1 tbsp of maize while the water comes to a boil.
- Keep stirring the mixture well to avoid lumps, even as the mixture thickens.
- The mixture will begin to come away from the sides of the pan.
- Allow it to cook for 2 or 3 minutes.
- At this point, either transfer the Ugali to a platter from the pan. Place the plate over the pan and turn it upside down or transfer to a small heat proof bowl.
- Pat it down to shape.
- Place a plate over the bowl and turn it over.
- Enjoy piping hot Ugali with your favorite stew or curry.

Doce Bhaji from the Grao Family

Ingredients

1. 250 gms, broken wheat
2. 1 coconut for the milk
3. 100 gm sugar (the lesser, the better)
4. 1 spoon of ghee
5. 1 spoon Nutmeg powder
6. 6 pcs of cardamom
7. Salt to taste

Method

- Use three bricks (the older, the better) and light a fire under it.
- Place the frying pan over the bricks to heat them.
- Add the broken wheat previously immersed in water for a few hours.
- Stir the soaked broken wheat and water continuously with the wooden ladle (dovlo).
- Stir and stir till it reaches a thick consistency.
- As it thickens, add cashew nuts, dried grapes, a small drop of ghee, and cardamom powder. Continue to stir and enjoy the aroma. But watch out.
- When it is almost ready, the sides will part from the pan.
- Pour it in a well-greased serving tray and top it off with a few cashew nuts. Allow it to cool and it's ready to be enjoyed with the entire family.

Apa de Painço- Thick Millet tortilla

"I have been preparing this dish for my children. Maria Emilia, my mother-in-law, passed it to me when I entered her family with an advice that "Gorcheak gott kor", ever since my family prepare this - Antoinette"

Ingredients

1. Nachnem powder
2. Grated fresh coconut
3. Banana
4. Some Salt.

Instructions

- Soak the Millet powder overnight.
- On a grinding stone, grind the grated coconut to a fine consistency.
- Mix all ingredients and the mashed banana.
- Make sure you don't add much water.
- Take a clean banana leaf,
- Keep a tawa on the flame, put the banana leaf on the tawa,
- Spread the dough on the leaf and make a round thick chapatti,
- Cover the tawa and let it roast well.
- When ready, serve it hot with lemongrass black tea and enjoy with family and friends.

"Mind you, your neighbours will rush to eat this as the aroma is powerful and travels far. - Antoinette"

Sannas de jaca-Jackfruit Sannas

"I think this is an almost forgotten dish, but Dr. Gwendolyn's family still prepares it, and I relish the sannas whenever she gets some for me. - Antoinette"

Ingredients

1. 250 gms ukde (Goan parboiled) rice.
2. 1 grated fresh coconut.
3. 750ml coconut toddy.
4. Salt.
5. Ripe jackfruit bulbs.

Instructions

- Clean, wash, and soak ukde rice overnight.
- Grind it fine using coconut toddy.
- Grind the grated coconut with toddy.
- Mix the ground rice and coconut.
- Add salt to taste.
- Stir with coconut toddy to form a thick batter.
- Keep covered in the sun or fireplace until it ferments and doubles up in quantity.
- Chop the ripe jackfruit bulbs into tiny cubes and mix them into the batter.
- Pour into the sannas moulds, get the kompro ready with water at the bottom, place the moulds for steaming for about 20 minutes until firm.
- Test with a knife to check if the jaca sannas are ready.
- If the knife comes clean, there, it's ready.
- Enjoy the sannas at hi-tea with your family and neighbours.

A Book For Mum On Her Birthday

The Maichem Fest marked a memorable celebration of family heritage with the soft launch of a book that beautifully encapsulates the life of Antoinette Fernandes, a remarkable figure who has touched many lives across three continents. Festecar Marius Fernandes, known for his dedication to organizing community festivals in Goa, honoured his mother, Antoinette, on her birthday at their family home in Amboi Vaddo , São Mathias, Divar, by introducing a publication titled "Across Three Continents: The Legacy of Antonette Fernandes."

The book recounts Antoinette's life journey from her roots in Goa, her adventurous years in Laare, Kenya, and later, her influential time in Leicester, UK. It highlights her work in helping raise funds to build a church in Kenya, organizing the first Alfred

Rose tiatr in the UK in 1986, and her efforts in preserving Goan culture, particularly the Konkani language, across the globe.

Marius expressed that the book not only celebrates Antoinette's extraordinary life but also preserves their family's heritage for future generations. He emphasized the importance of documenting memories and efforts as a way to honor and remember those who came before.

Nicole Suares, shared how Antonette's stories, gathered over the past decade, were a source of inspiration and joy and expressed her delight in capturing her legacy.

Dr. Gwendolyn de Ornelas praised Antoinette as an inspiration to the Goan diaspora, particularly noting her significant contributions to the world through her resilience and spirit.

Miguel Braganza, a friend of the family, also lauded Antonetta's warm hospitality and her unwavering dedication to keeping Goan traditions alive, wherever she went.

The book launch at the Maichem Fest became not only a tribute to a matriarch but a celebration of Goan culture, family and the power of storytelling across generations.

www.ingramcontent.com/pod-product-compliance
Lightning Source LLC
Chambersburg PA
CBHW040910110726
48005CB00006B/865